CAT PHYSICS

BY MENDENHALL

C=AT²

A CARTOON PRIMER

HarperPerennial

A Division of HarperCollins*Publishers*

HarperCollins books may be purchased for educational, business, or sales promotional use. For information please write: Special Markets Department, HarperCollins Publishers, Inc., 10 East 53rd Street, New York, NY 10022.

FIRST EDITION

Designed by Kim Llewellyn

LIBRARY OF CONGRESS CATALOG CARD NUMBER 92-56250

ISBN 0-06-095000-5

93 94 95 96 97 CW 10 9 8 7 6 5 4 3 2 1

ACKNOWLEDGMENTS

I WISH TO THANK MY WIFE MARY FOR HER TIRELESS LOVE AND ENCOURAGEMENT, AND FOR TEACHING ME IT'S OK TO BE IMPERFECT. SPECIAL THANKS TO JUDI SCHULER WHOSE REMARKABLE ENERGY AND PERSISTENCE MADE THE BOOK POSSIBLE. OF COURSE, MY THANKS TO TIGER, SUGAR AND BLACKIE WHO TAUGHT ME ALL ABOUT CAT PHYSICS, SERVED AS UNCOMPLAINING, UNDERPAID MODELS AND GAVE ME THEIR UNLIMITED LOVE.

TIGER   SUGAR   BLACKIE

ALTHOUGH THIS BOOK IS TITLED <u>CAT PHYSICS</u>, THE LAWS, PRINCIPLES, AXIOMS, POSTULATES AND THEOREMS PRESENTED ARE DRAWN FROM MANY RELATED DISCIPLINES, INCLUDING CAT CHEMISTRY, CAT BIOLOGY, CAT PSYCHOLOGY, CAT MEDICINE, CAT LOGIC, CAT HISTORY, CAT MATHEMATICS AND CAT ENGINEERING.

THE AUTHOR DOES NOT INTEND TO DIMINISH THE RICH CONTRIBUTIONS THESE RELATED DISCIPLINES HAVE MADE TO THE STUDY OF <u>CAT PHYSICS</u>.

G. A. MENDENHALL

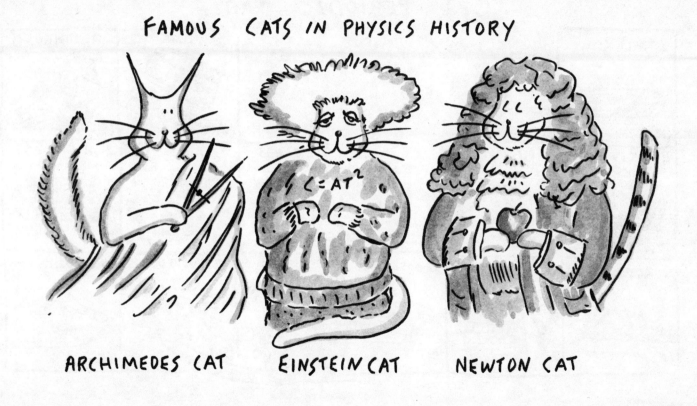

CAT PERIODIC TABLE

1 MILK		2 TUNA	3 BIRDS
MILK (M)		(T)	(B)
4 KITTY FOOD	5 ELECTRIC HEATING PADS	6 LIZARDS	7 YARN	8 SHOEBOXES
NUMMIES FOR JUMMIES (Kf)	(Ep)		(Y)	(Sb)
9 RODENTS	10 ICE CREAM (AN ISOTOPE OF MILK)	11 SOFT BEDS	TOYS	13 THE SUN	14 BRUSHES
(R)	VANILLA (Ic)	(S)		(Su)	(Br)

LAW OF CAT INERTIA

A CAT AT REST WILL TEND TO REMAIN AT REST — UNLESS ACTED UPON BY SOME OUTSIDE FORCE.

LAW OF CAT MOTION

A CAT WILL MOVE IN A STRAIGHT LINE — UNLESS THERE IS
SOME REALLY GOOD REASON TO CHANGE DIRECTION.

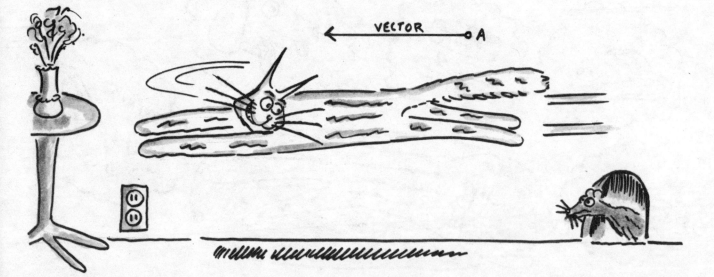

LAW OF CAT MAGNETISM

ALL BLUE BLAZERS AND BLACK SWEATERS ATTRACT CAT HAIR IN DIRECT PROPORTION TO THE DARKNESS OF THE FABRIC.

LAW OF CAT THERMODYNAMICS

HEAT FLOWS FROM A WARMER TO A COOLER BODY— EXCEPT
IN THE CASE OF A CAT— ALL HEAT FLOWS TO THE CAT.

HEAT

LAW OF CAT STRETCHING

A CAT WILL STRETCH TO A DISTANCE PROPORTIONAL TO THE LENGTH OF THE NAP JUST TAKEN.

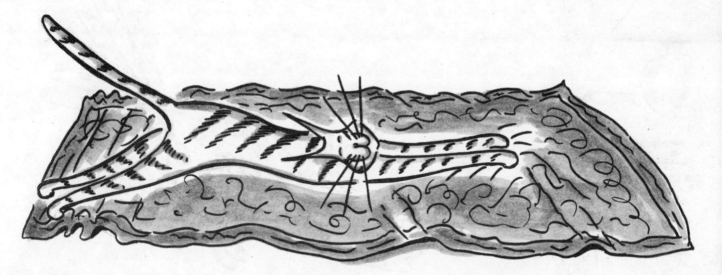

LAW OF CAT CONCENTRATION

A CAT'S CONCENTRATION WILL VARY IN DIRECT RELATION TO HIS INTEREST IN ANY GIVEN SUBJECT.

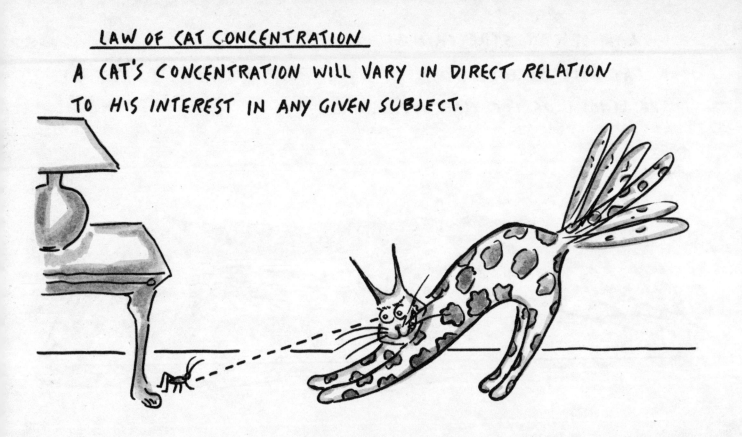

LAW OF CAT ACCELERATION

A CAT WILL ACCELERATE AT A CONSTANT SPEED—UNTIL HE GETS <u>GOOD</u> AND <u>READY</u> TO STOP.

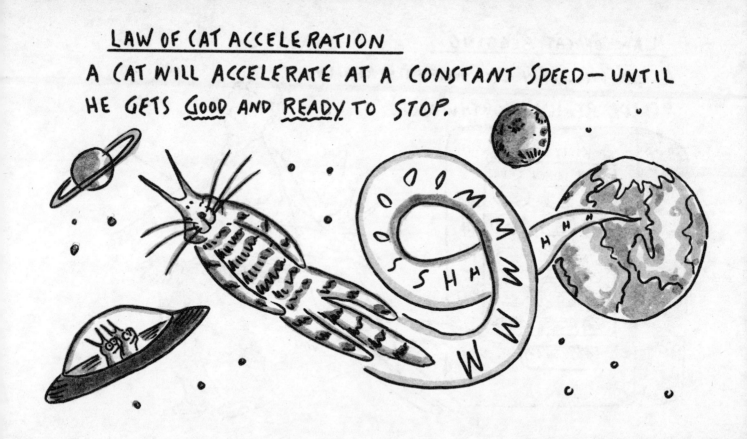

LAW OF RUG CONFIGURATION

NO RUG MAY REMAIN IN ITS NATURALLY FLAT STATE — FOR VERY DARN LONG.

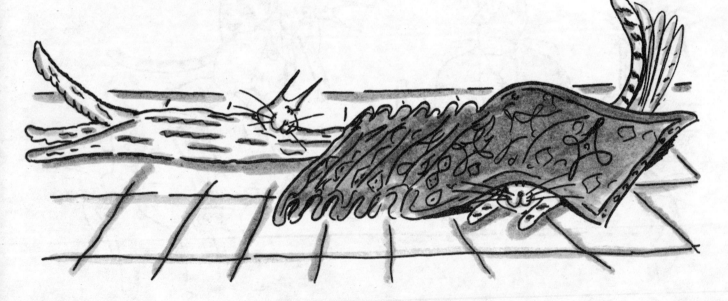

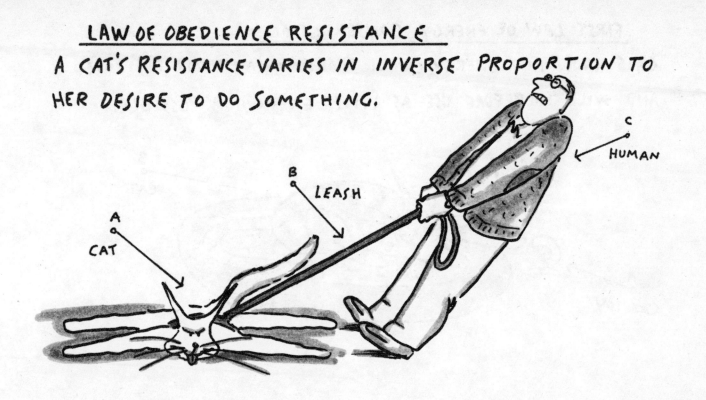

FIRST LAW OF ENERGY CONSERVATION

CATS KNOW THAT ENERGY CAN NEITHER BE CREATED NOR DESTROYED AND WILL THEREFORE USE AS LITTLE ENERGY AS POSSIBLE.

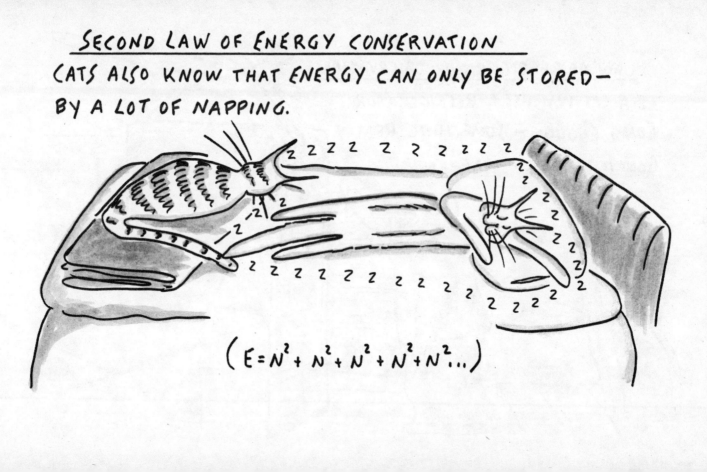

LAW OF ELECTRIC BLANKET ATTRACTION

TURN ON AN ELECTRIC BLANKET, AND A CAT WILL JUMP INTO BED AT THE SPEED OF LIGHT.

CLICK

LAW OF RANDOM COMFORT SEEKING

A CAT WILL ALWAYS SEEK, AND USUALLY TAKE OVER, THE MOST COMFORTABLE SPOT IN ANY GIVEN ROOM.

FIRST LAW OF CAT BATHING

A CAT WILL TAKE A BATH ANYTIME AND ANYWHERE IT SEEMS CONVENIENT.

LAW OF ULTRALOW TEMPERATURES

A CAT REACHING ABSOLUTE ZERO WILL INSIST ON A HEATING PAD, A FIREPLACE AND A WARM LAP—IMMEDIATELY.

LAW OF SPACE OCCUPANCY

ALL BAGS IN A GIVEN ROOM MUST CONTAIN A CAT WITHIN THE EARLIEST POSSIBLE NANOSECOND.

E — JEALOUS CAT

D — CAT

B — CAT

A — SHOPPING BAG

C — GROCERY BAG

LAW OF UNIT MEASUREMENT

ONE CAT FOOT POUND IS THE AMOUNT OF WORK NEEDED TO LIFT ONE POUND ONE FOOT — BUT CATS NEVER WORK.

LAW OF CIRCULAR MOTION

A CAT WILL FOLLOW AN OBJECT MOVING IN A FIXED CIRCULAR PATH— AND HER TAIL WILL DO THE SAME.

A → CAT

B → OBJECT

C → OTHER TOYS

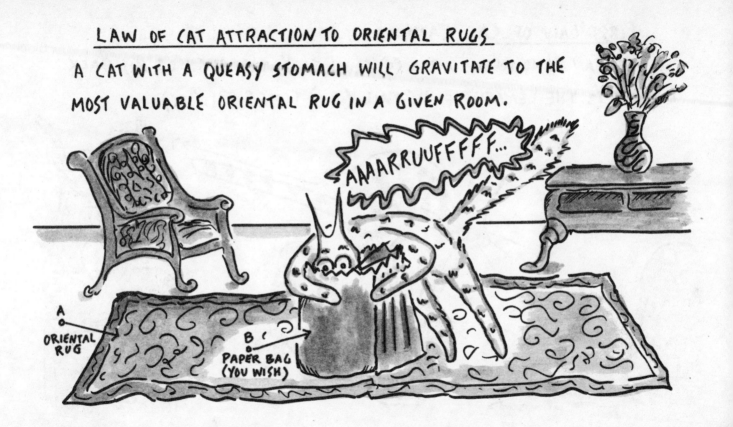

FIRST LAW OF CAT LANDING

A CAT CAN LAND IN AN AREA (C) EQUAL TO ⅓ THE ARCH OF HIS BACK (AX) OR ⅓ THE LENGTH OF HIS TAIL (BY) TIMES PI (π).

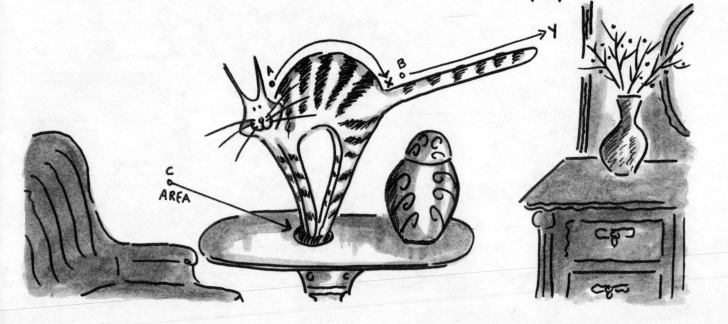

LAW OF FLUID DISPLACEMENT

A CAT IMMERSED IN MILK WILL DISPLACE HER OWN VOLUME—MINUS THE AMOUNT OF MILK CONSUMED.

C
CAT

B
SMALL MILK BOWL

A
BIG MILK BOWL

MILK

MILK

LAW OF CAT DISINTEREST

A CAT'S INTEREST LEVEL OFTEN VARIES IN INVERSE PROPORTION TO THE AMOUNT OF EFFORT YOU EXPEND.

FIRST LAW OF TAIL ANGLES

THE ANGLE OF A CAT'S TAIL WILL EQUAL OR EXCEED 90° WHEN HE'S CONTENT, AND WILL BE LESS THAN 90° WHEN HE'S NOT.

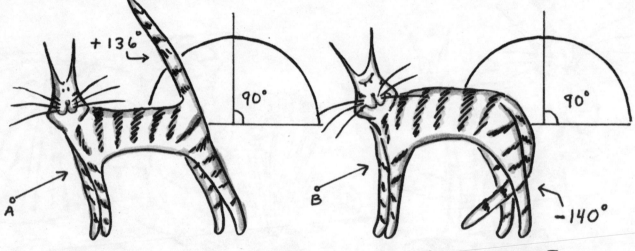

+136°

90°

A

CONTENT

B

90°

−140°

NOT SO CONTENT

SECOND LAW OF TAIL ANGLES

WHEN A CAT'S TAIL IS THE HYPOTENUSE OF A RIGHT TRIANGLE, ITS LENGTH IS THE SUM OF THE SQUARES OF THE OTHER TWO SIDES OR $AB^2 + BC^2 = AC^2$.

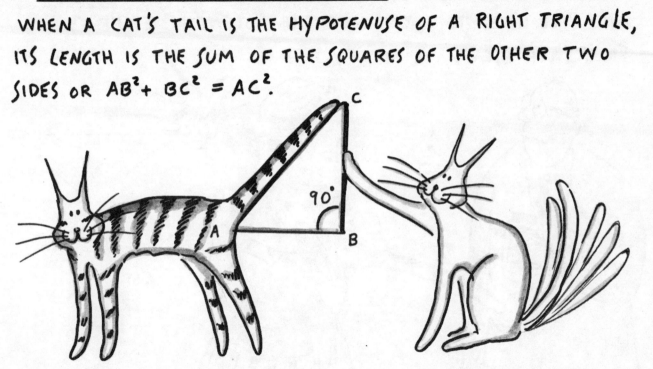

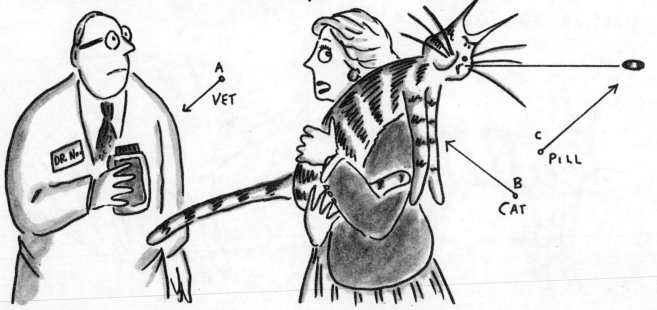

LAW OF SHOT AVOIDANCE

A CAT WILL DO JUST ABOUT ANYTHING TO AVOID A SHOT.

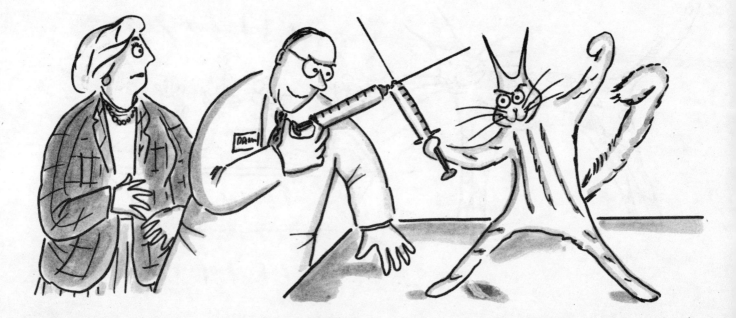

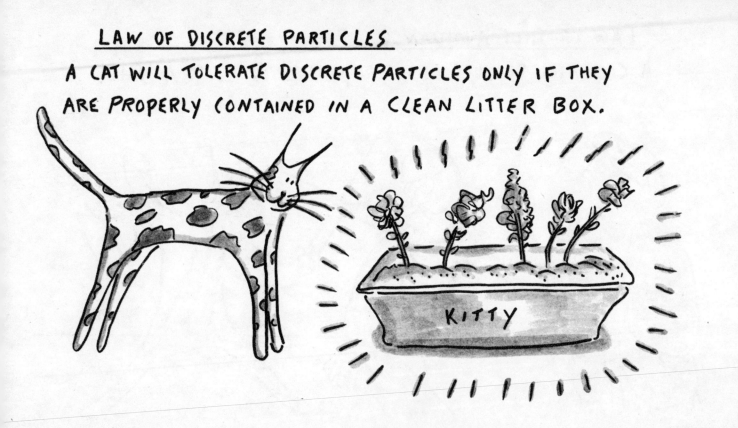

LAW OF CAT COMPOSITION

CATS ARE COMPOSED OF THE FOLLOWING:

  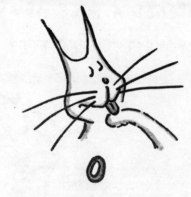

MATTER   ANTI-MATTER AND IT DOESN'T MATTER

LAW OF EQUIDISTANT SEPARATION

ALL CATS IN A GIVEN ROOM WILL LOCATE AT POINTS EQUIDISTANT FROM EACH OTHER, AND EQUIDISTANT FROM THE CENTER OF THE ROOM.

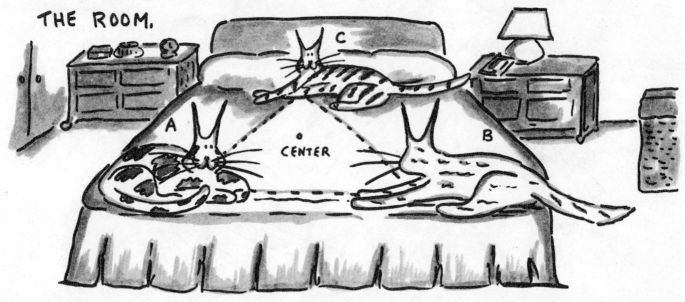

LAW OF CAT NIGHT VISION

A CAT CAN SEE IN THE DARK—AND YOU CAN'T.

BOINK

LAW OF CHAIN REACTION

WHEN A SMALL, FURRY ANIMAL (C) TRAVELS IN A CONTINUOUS PATH BETWEEN CAT A AND CAT B, THE REACTION IS SELF-SUSTAINING.

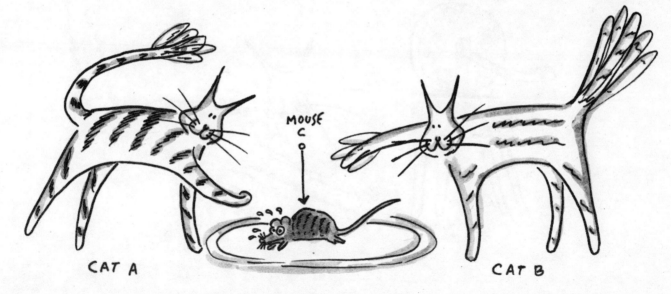

MOUSE C

CAT A

CAT B

LAW OF CLAW SHARPENING

ALL CLAWS MUST BE SHARPENED TO THE LAST POSSIBLE
NUCLEUS OF THE LAST POSSIBLE ATOM.

LAW OF CAT DIGNITY

ALL CATS MAINTAIN THE MAXIMUM AMOUNT OF GRACE
AND DIGNITY—NO MATTER WHAT THE SITUATION.

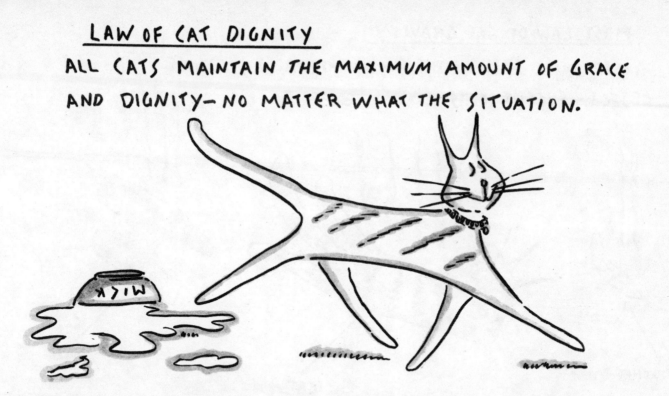

FIRST LAW OF CAT GRAVITY

A CAT WILL FALL AT THE SAME RATE AS ANY OTHER OBJECT—EXCEPT CATS HARDLY EVER FALL.

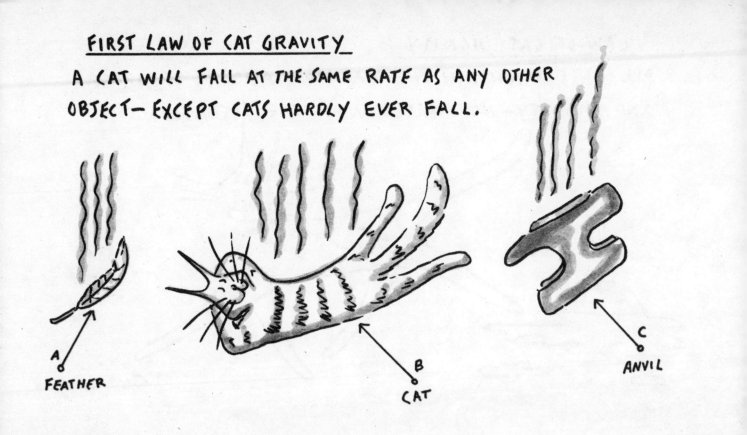

A
FEATHER

B
CAT

C
ANVIL

SECOND LAW OF CAT GRAVITY

ALL CATS ARE EXEMPT FROM THE ORDINARY LAWS OF GRAVITY.

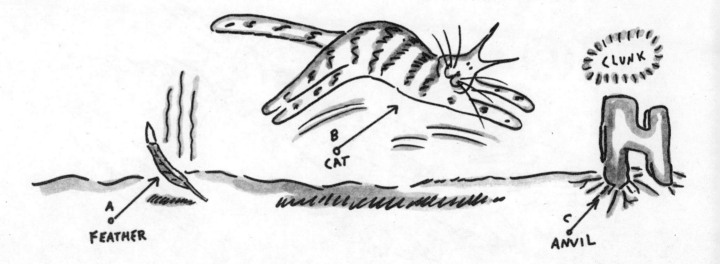

SPECIAL LAW OF MASS AND VELOCITY

A CAT TRAVELING AT OR NEAR THE SPEED OF LIGHT WILL BECOME GEOMETRICALLY MORE MASSIVE — UNLESS HE IS ON A REALLY GOOD DIET.

SPACE-TIME CONTINUUM

GIVEN ENOUGH TIME, A CAT WILL LAND IN JUST ABOUT ANY SPACE.

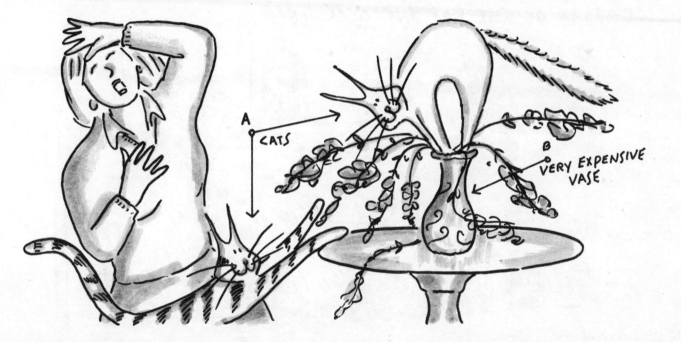

LAW OF CONCENTRATION OF MASS

A CAT'S MASS INCREASES IN DIRECT PROPORTION TO THE COMFORT OF THE LAP *SHE* OCCUPIES.

LAW OF CAT PROPORTION

THE ARCH OF A CAT'S BACK IS EQUAL TO THE DISTANCE BETWEEN HIS FEET DIVIDED BY PI UNLESS...

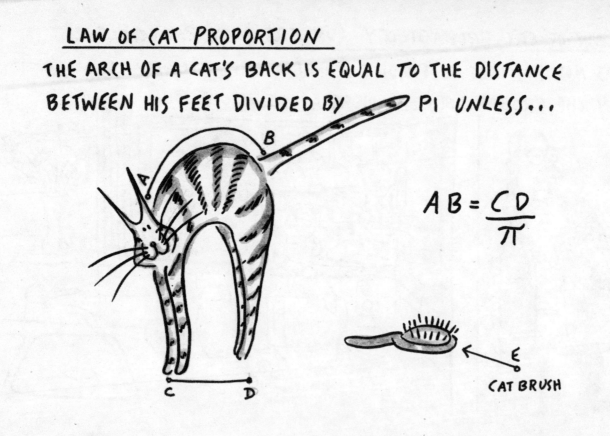

$$AB = \frac{CD}{\pi}$$

CAT BRUSH

THAT CAT IS ENJOYING A FABULOUS BRUSHING.

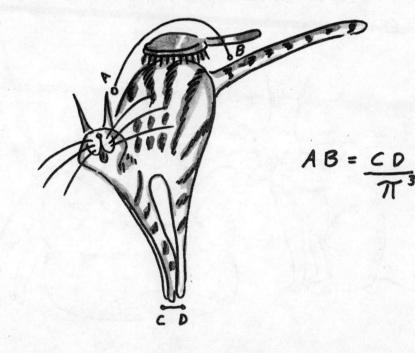

$$AB = \frac{CD}{\pi^3}$$

WAVE THEORY

IT'S IMPOSSIBLE TO TEACH A CAT TO WAVE BYE-BYE.

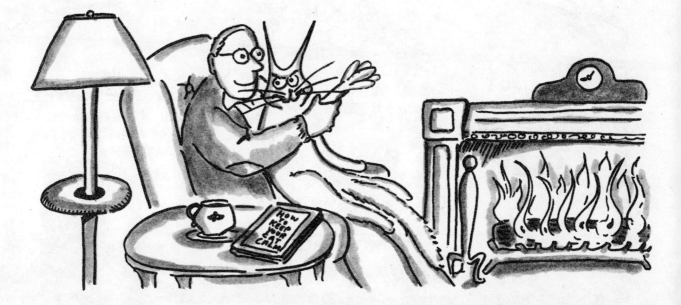